A-MAZE-ING ADVENTURES
FUN FINGER MAZES

BY JILL KALZ   ILLUSTRATED BY MATTIA CERATO

PICTURE WINDOW BOOKS
a capstone imprint

A-MAZE-ING ADVENTURES
FUN FINGER MAZES

BY JILL KALZ

ILLUSTRATED BY MATTIA CERATO

PICTURE WINDOW BOOKS
a capstone imprint

Table of Contents

Answers start on page 104.

For added difficulty, try finding all the characters you see here!

AN A-MAZE-ING AMUSEMENT PARK ADVENTURE

WELCOME TO THE
A-MAZE-ING
AMUSEMENT PARK

Here's what you do: Use your finger to make your way through each maze from start to finish. If a person, tree, or other object blocks your way, choose a different path. It's **OK** to use the slides and stairways. You can go through the archways too. The star in the lower left corner of each maze shows direction. It's called a compass rose. The boxes with tiny pictures are called keys or legends. They'll help you find snack shacks, restrooms, shopping, and more.

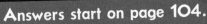

What's that sneaky clown up to?
See if you can spot him in each maze.

Answers start on page 104.

FINISH

STORE

ATM

KNIGHT'S DINER

RING TOSS

POP-IT

START

FINISH

JUNGLE BOAT JAM

CANDY SHOP

HOUSE of SCARE

KEY

	Dining		First Aid
	Shopping		Information
	Restrooms		ATM

9

START

10

START

Mr. Bobo's Fun House

Time to get silly! Is the clown in the red pants west or east of the slide? Which direction is he from the mirrors? You enter the green hedge maze on its west side, but on what side do you exit? Can you find all 19 people with black hair?

FINISH

START

14

MAZE-o-saurus!

Feel the earth rumble. Hear the dinosaurs grumble. The volcanoes are starting to blow! Can you find the four cameras? Is the giant gray apatosaurus west or east of the smoking volcano? North or south of the tar pit?

FINISH

15

Jungle Boat Jam

Float through the jungles of the world and see how many animals you can name. Which direction are the hippos from the elephant? Are the spotted leopards north or south of the tall stone temple?

START

JUNGLE BOAT JAM

FINISH

LittleLand

Little rides are big fun! Is the Ferris wheel west or east of the ice cream stand? Which building is west of the restrooms? Can you spot all five trash cans? Use the key to find the first-aid hut and the **ATM**.

18

FINISH

KEY

Dining

First Aid

Shopping

Information

Restrooms

ATM

CANDY SHOP

19

START

DOCTOR SHOCKER

20

Doctor Shocker

Want to give your heart a shock? Hop onboard, and hold on tight! There are no wrong turns, just one wild ride. Is the stethoscope north or south of the compass rose? Which direction is the finish from the start?

FINISH

House of Scare

What kinds of spooky creatures lurk inside this maze? Which direction is the mummy from the vampire? How many torches hang on the walls? The bat sign is on which side of the house, north or south?

START

HOUSE OF SCARE

FINISH

START

24

Redline Speedway

It's a race to the finish, but watch out for the roadblocks! Is car 8 west or east of car 3? On which side of the speedway is the food stand? What building is north of the restrooms? Can you find all 31 spare tires?

FINISH

KEY

- ⊗ Dining
- ✛ First Aid
- 🛍 Shopping
- $ ATM
- 👥 Restrooms

START

26

Ker-PLASH!

Only one of these wacky water slides is a winner. Can you find it? Is the empty pool north or south of the finish? Which direction is the dirty pool from the compass rose? Should the boy carrying the dark-purple inner tube walk north or south to get to the start?

FINISH

Lucky Lane

Shoot a basket. Pop a balloon. Hit the bull's-eye and win a prize! Which building is east of the banana game? How many gift shops can you spot? Is the ring toss west or east of the duck game?

BEAN BAG TOSS

START

ATM

STORE

BANA

100

RING TOSS

POP-IT

KNIGHT'S DINER

FINISH

KEY

Dining

Information

Shopping

ATM

Restrooms

29

AN A-MAZE-ING FARM ADVENTURE

START

FINISH

WELCOME TO THE

A-MAZE-ING FARM

Here's what you do: Use your finger to make your way through each maze from start to finish. If a person, tree, or other object blocks your way, choose a different path. It's **OK** to use the bridges and ladders. The star in the lower left corner of each maze shows direction. It's called a compass rose. The boxes with tiny pictures are called keys or legends. They'll help you find barns, chicken coops, wagon rides, and more.

What's that silly dog up to? See if you can spot him sneaking through each maze.

Answers start on page 110.

31

START

32

On the Farm

Time for chores! First, use the key to find the chicken coop, and collect the eggs. Next, find the grain bins, and gather lunch for the cows. Is the greenhouse west or east of the farmer's house? North or south of the two apple-pickers?

KEY

- Barn
- Greenhouse
- Chicken Coop
- House
- Grain

FINISH

Corn Confusion

Keeping the critters out of the corn is a full-time job. Are the three raccoons west or east of the Finish? Which direction is the running deer from the compass rose? Can you spot the three pitchforks?

START

Ponies in a Pickle

The ponies are puzzled. Can you find your way through these fences? Which building is farthest south? Farthest east? Is the training area north or south of the boy flying a kite?

START

36

FINISH

KEY

Barn

Machine Shed

House

Training Area

Grain

37

Tulip Tangle

Walk, skip, or tiptoe through the tulips! How many bridges are west of the Start? How many are east? Can you find the four people without a flower basket?

START

38

START

Hey, Hey! It's Hay!

Raise the barn roof, and peek inside. Use the key to find the tack room. It holds all the horse-riding gear. Which direction are the cows from the hay loft? Can you spot all six metal pails?

FINISH

KEY

Hay Loft

Workshop

Tack Room

START

42

Roundabout Rice

What grows in this soggy field? Rice! Stick to the skinny green path from the Start sign to the Finish sign. And be sure to wave at the 11 water buffalo. Is the compass rose north or south of the biggest hut? Which direction is the dog from that hut?

FINISH

START

44

Lost in Lavender

Ahhh ... this field of purple flowers smells like perfume! Most of the lavender pickers have filled their baskets. But can you spot the 10 empty baskets? Is the man wearing a cap west or east of the woman wearing a bright pink shirt?

FINISH

Ziggy Zaggy Piggies

Can you wiggle around these pigs without wallowing in the mud? Which direction is the boy in the red shirt from the woman in the yellow shirt? Which direction is she from the dog? The Start? The sun?

46

START

48

Dairy Farm Detour

Mmm-morning! These dairy cows are ready to be mmm-milked! Which is farther west—the milking parlor or the tanker trucks? If you're standing by the Finish, which direction do you have to go to get to the bulk tanks?

FINISH

KEY

C Computer

Milking Parlor

Bulk Tank

Tanker Truck

Pumpkin Patch Puzzle

Pose with a scarecrow. Catch the beat of the local band. Share some fall festival food. And whoop it up on a wagon ride. Which direction are the gift shops from the ticket booth? Can you find all nine sunflowers?

BIGGEST

START

50

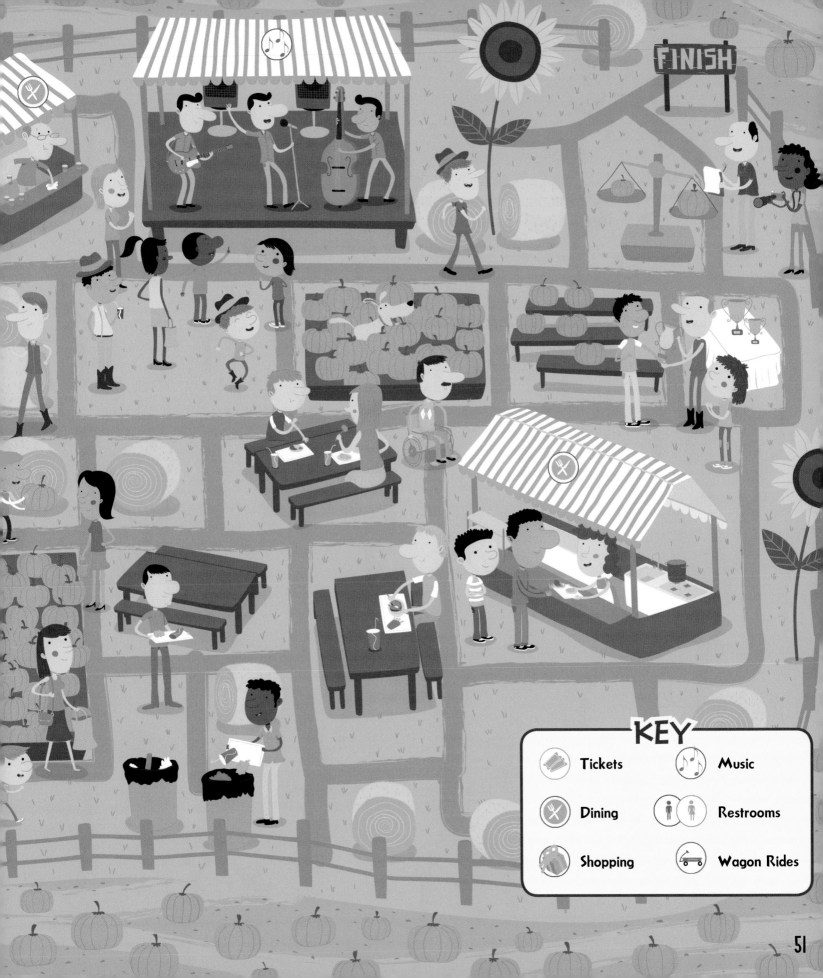

KEY

Tickets   Music

Dining   Restrooms

Shopping   Wagon Rides

FINISH

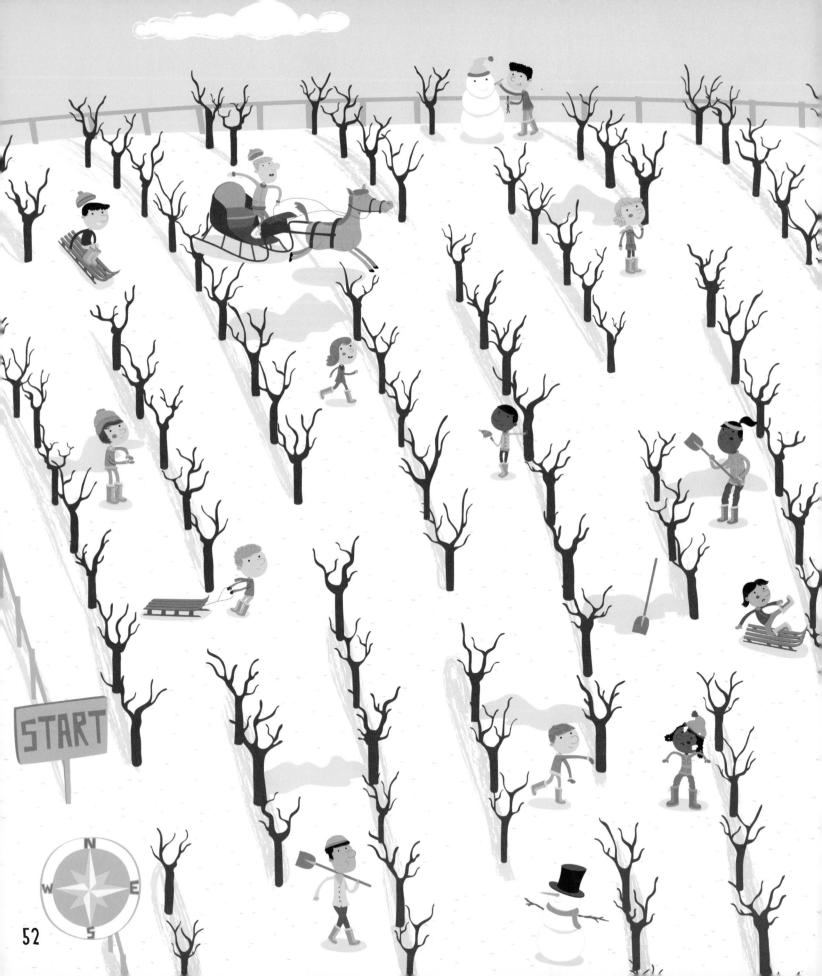

START

52

Baffled by Apple Trees

Apple trees sleep all winter—and they miss all the snowy fun! Is the two-person sleigh west or east of the snowmen? West or east of the compass rose? See if you can find the seven sleds.

FINISH

AN A-MAZE-ING SCHOOL ADVENTURE

WELCOME TO THE
A-MAZE-ING SCHOOL

Here's what you do: Use your finger to make your way through each maze from start to finish. If a person, chair, or other object blocks your way, choose a different path. It's **OK** to use the stairs and ladders. The star in the lower left corner of each maze shows direction. It's called a compass rose. The boxes with tiny pictures are called keys or legends. They'll help you find art supplies, books, field day events, and more.

What's that frisky guinea pig up to? See if you can spot him sneaking through each maze.

Answers start on page 116.

Hooray for Homeroom!

Can you find your way through this mess of desks? Which direction is the Start door from the Finish door? Is the globe north or south of the pink backpack? Can you spot the other six backpacks?

START

START

HOT!

58

Read All about It

Discover magic in the media center—but quietly, please! Use the key to find the fiction, nonfiction, and reference book sections. Are the audio/visual cases north or south of the storyteller? West or east of the games?

START

FINISH

KEY

(F) Fiction (headphones) Audio/Visual

(NF) Nonfiction (magazines) Magazines

(R) Reference (mouse) Computer Catalog

(Games) Games (book) Circulation Desk

61

Balls, Walls, Nets, and Beams

Time to tumble and twist. Catch and climb. Bounce, balance, and bump. If you're standing at the volleyball net, which direction should you go to get to the climbing wall? To the yellow beams? Can you find all 21 balls? (And don't worry; you *can* cross the white lines on the floor to get to the Finish!)

START

FINISH

63

Take Your Seat

Lots of empty seats in the auditorium, but only one is yours. Once you get to the Finish, see if you can spot the two students taking a nap.

Who's Hungry?

Is that your stomach growling? Let's eat! Is the lunch counter west or east of the recycling bins? Which direction are the trash bins from the boy with the football? Can you find the nine tables that have just one student?

Finish

KEY

🍎 Lunch Counter   ♻ Recycling

🗑 Trash   TR Tray Return

START

68

Field Day Frazzle

Get ready ... get set ... GO! If you're standing by the sign-up table, which direction do you have to go to get to the long jump? The obstacle course? The compass rose? Are the tug-of-war kids pulling north and south, or west and east?

FINISH

KEY

- Sign-up Table
- Obstacle Course
- Award Stage
- 50-yard Dash
- Long Jump
- Tug-of-war

Baffled in Band

Make some music! TOODLE-E-DOO! How many instruments can you name? Can you spot all 11 drums? Is the piano west or east of the Start? Which is farther south—the guitar or the harp?

START

CLAY

74

The Heart of Art

Draw a daisy. Play with clay. What will you paint today? Use the key to find all five pottery stations. Which direction are they from the art supplies? Is the key north or south of the cleanup area?

FINISH

KEY

- Art Supplies
- Cleanup Area
- Kiln
- Pottery Station

START

76

Take a Bow!

The school play is just days away, and there's still so much to do! Are the costume racks west or east of the painters? Which is farther north—the car or the five-eyed monster? Can you find all 10 stage lights?

FINISH

START

AN A-MAZE-ING ZOO ADVENTURE

WELCOME TO THE

A-MAZE-ING ZOO

Here's what you do: Use your finger to make your way through each maze from start to finish. If a person, tree, or other object blocks your way, choose a different path. It's **OK** to use the bridges and stairways. The star in the lower left corner of each maze shows direction. It's called a compass rose. The boxes with tiny pictures are called keys or legends. They'll help you find snack shacks, restrooms, shopping, and more.

What's that silly monkey up to? See if you can spot him sneaking through each maze.

Answers start on page 122.

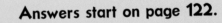

SOUVENIR

INFO

FOOD

START

80

Who's at the Zoo?

Look at all these animals! How many different kinds can you find?
Which animals are east of the kangaroos? North of the penguins?
Use the key to find the three gift shops.

FINISH

NURSERY

LIGHTS OUT

POLAR SHOP

IGLOO CAFE

LOST/FOUND

KEY

Dining		Animal Feeder	
Shopping		Lockers	
Restrooms		Photo Spot	
Information		First Aid	
ATM		Lost and Found	

Outback Odyssey

From cuddly koala bears to wacky wombats, Outback Odyssey is home to animals from Australia. What building is west of the black Tasmanian devils? Can you spot the nine balloons? The five people with orange hair?

FINISH

FOOD

CLOSED

KEY

Dining

Restrooms

Shopping

Information

83

The Asia Trail

It's a jumbled jungle out here! Can you find all three information signs? Which animals are east of the gift shop? If you're standing by the bats, which direction do you have to go to see the turtle pool?

START

84

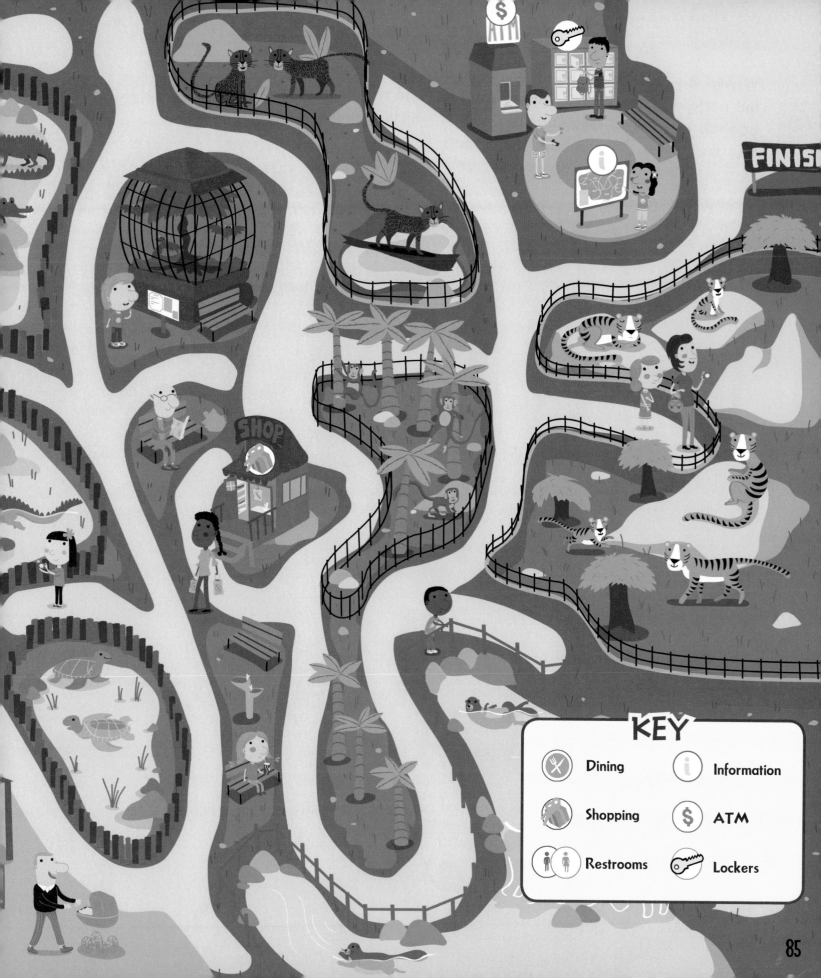

FINISH

KEY

Dining · Information

Shopping · ATM

Restrooms · Lockers

SHOP

ATM

African Safari

Whew! It's hot! Cool off with some ice cream. Is the dining hut north or south of the hippos? Can you find all five fat baobab trees? The elephants are east of which animals? Use the key to find the best photo spot.

START

GIFTS

SHOP

DINING

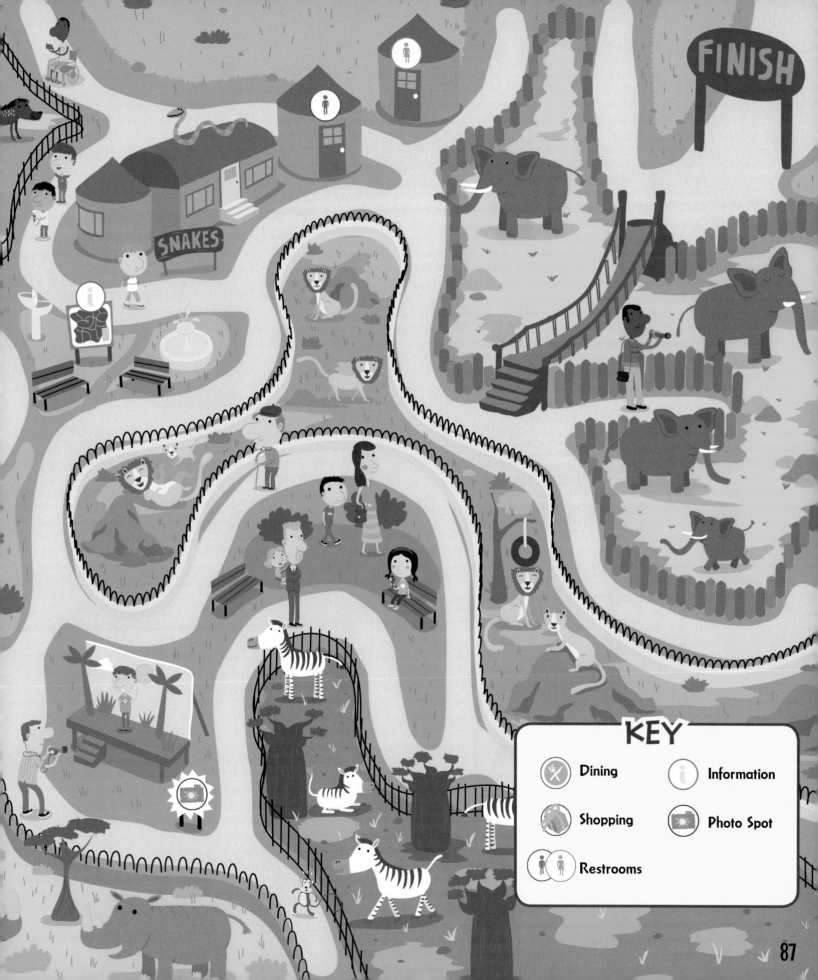

FINISH

SNAKES

KEY

🍴 Dining

🛍️ Shopping

🚻 Restrooms

ℹ️ Information

📷 Photo Spot

START

88

Discovery Island: Reptile House

Creep, crawl, and slither from start to finish. How many snakes can you find? Are the alligator and crocodiles west or east of the sea turtles? Which direction are the curly-tailed chameleons from the sleeping man?

FINISH

START

90

Discovery Island: Lights Out!

Too dark to see? Not for the skunks, ocelots, and other nighttime creatures that live here! Which animals are the farthest north? Are the owls west or east of the water fountain? Can you spot all six people wearing green shirts?

FINISH

Discovery Island: On the Farm

The petting zoo can be quite a puzzle! Which animals are south of the mini horses? Are the sheep west or east of the ducks? Which direction are the butterflies from the bunnies? Use the key to find all three animal feeders.

START

NURSERY

FINISH

DINER

KEY

🍴 Dining   ⓘ Information

🚻 Restrooms   🌽 Animal Feeder

93

START

94

Polar Play

Filled with chilly thrills and icy surprises, Polar Play is a cool spot. How many information signs are there? Which building is west of the walruses? Are the caribou (reindeer) north or south of the arctic foxes?

FINISH

POLAR SHOP

IGLOO CAFE

KEY

Dining   Restrooms

Shopping   Information

95

Rain Forest Aviary and Monkey Land

Chirp! Chirp! Squawk, squawk! Squeal! Welcome to the noisiest part of the zoo! Can you find the seven benches? All 23 monkeys? If you're standing by the restrooms, which direction do you have to go to get to the Lost and Found?

FINISH

KEY

Dining

Information

Shopping

First Aid

Restrooms

Lost and Found

START

BOOK SIGNING

ZOO

ZOO

ZOO

DOG!!

ILLUSTRATOR
BOOK SIGNING

Shop Till You Drop

Before heading home, be sure to buy a zoo souvenir. Can you find all four giraffe snow globes? The four baseball caps? Which items are south of the lollipops—the purses or the books?

FINISH

Goodbye, Zoo!

There's only one way to the freeway. Find it before the traffic gets bad! Is the purple bus parked west or east of the motorcycles? What color is the car parked farthest north? Can you spot all three convertibles?

FINISH

MAZE ANSWERS

MAZE ANSWERS

A Day to Play (pages 8-9)

Ripple Rumble Roller Coaster (pages 10-11)

Mr. Bobo's Fun House (pages 12-13)

START

FINISH

MAZE-o-saurus! (pages 14-15)

START

FINISH

MAZE ANSWERS (continued)

Jungle Boat Jam (pages 16-17)

LittleLand (pages 18-19)

Doctor Shocker (pages 20-21)

START

DOCTOR SHOCKER

FINISH

House of Scare (pages 22-23)

FINISH

START

HOUSE of SCARE

MAZE ANSWERS (continued)

Redline Speedway (pages 24-25)

START

FINISH

Ker-PLASH! (pages 26-27)

START

FINISH

Lucky Lane (pages 28-29)

amusement:

something that makes you giggle, snicker, **smile,** snort, **cheer,** or chuckle

On the Farm
(pages 32-33)

Corn Confusion
(pages 34-35)

Ponies in a Pickle (pages 36-37)

Tulip Tangle (pages 38-39)

Hey, Hey! It's Hay! (pages 40-41)

Roundabout Rice (pages 42-43)

Lost in Lavender (pages 44-45)

Ziggy Zaggy Piggies (pages 46-47)

Dairy Farm Detour (pages 48-49)

Pumpkin Patch Puzzle (pages 50-51)

Baffled by Apple Trees

(pages 52-53)

MAZE ANSWERS (continued)

Hooray for Homeroom! (pages 56-57)

Lost in the Lab (pages 58-59)

Read All about It (pages 60-61)

Balls, Walls, Nets, and Beams (pages 62-63)

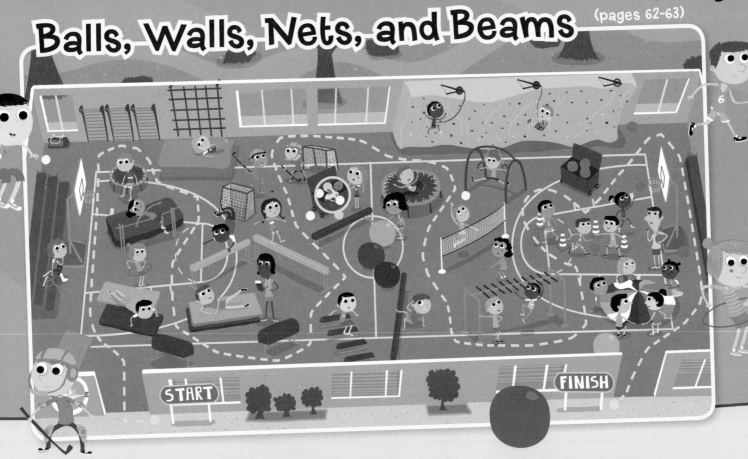

Take Your Seat (pages 64-65)

Who's Hungry? (pages 66-67)

Field Day Frazzle (pages 68-69)

Computer Confusion (pages 70-71)

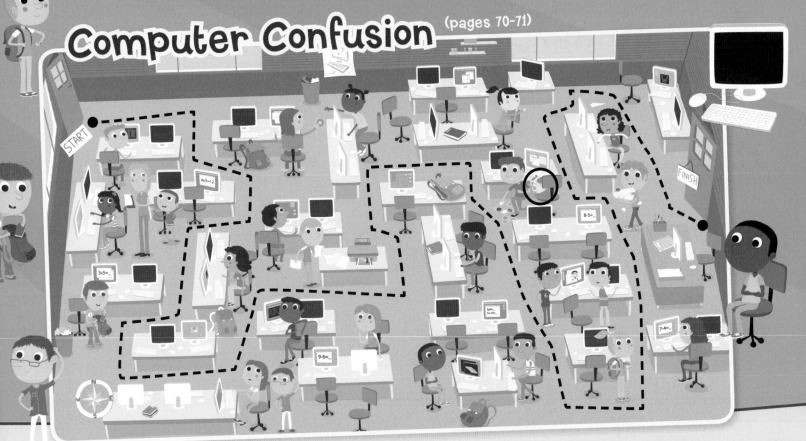

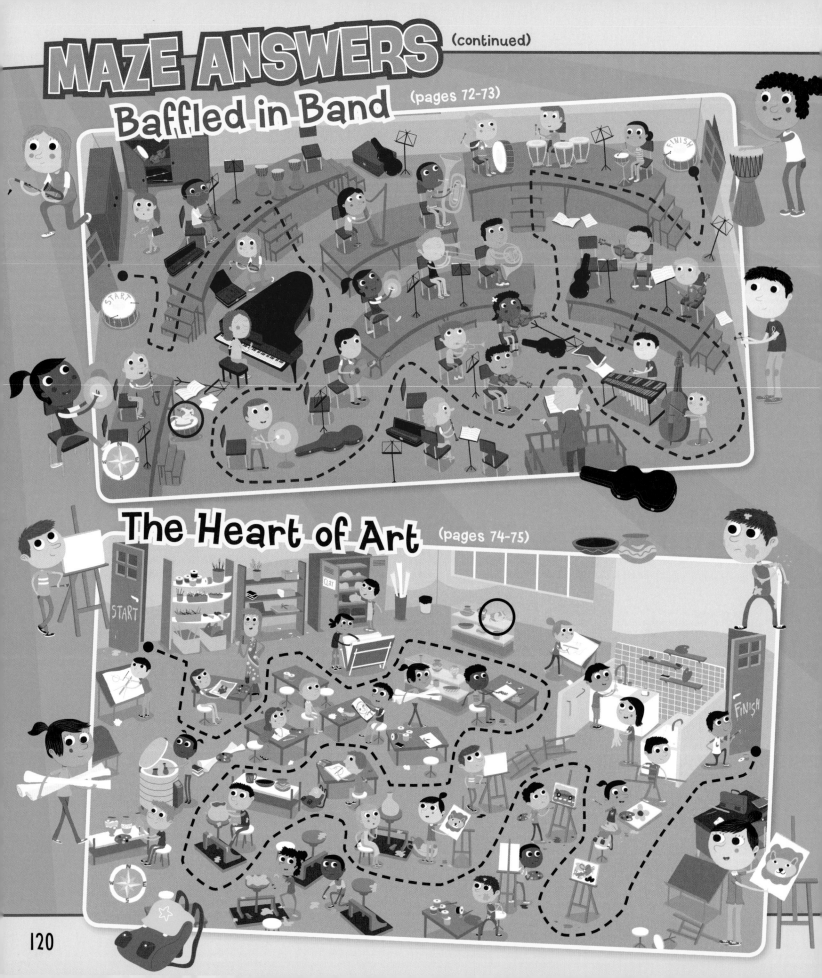

Baffled in Band (pages 72-73)

The Heart of Art (pages 74-75)

Take a Bow!

(pages 76-77)

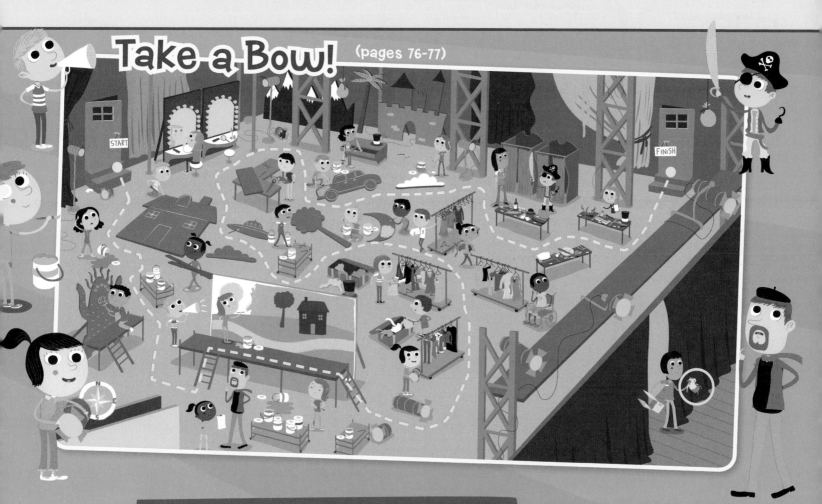

Guinea Pig Rules

1. Do not hide in backpacks.
2. Do not ride on book carts.
3. Do not hog all the balls.
4. Do not snack in the auditorium.
5. Do not jump on the drums.

Who's at the Zoo? (pages 80-81)

Outback Odyssey (pages 82-83)

The Asia Trail (pages 84-85)

African Safari (pages 86-87)

Discovery Island: Reptile House (pages 88-89)

Discovery Island: Lights Out! (pages 90-91)

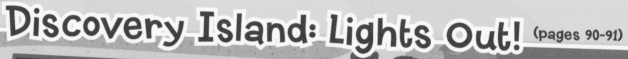

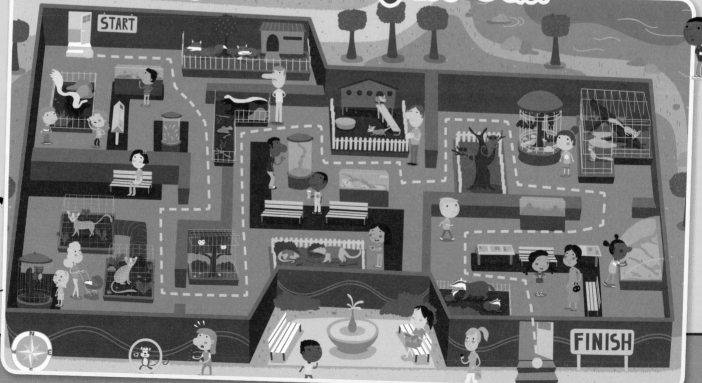

Discovery Island: On the Farm (pages 92-93)

Polar Play (pages 94-95)

Rain Forest Aviary and Monkey Land (pages 96-97)

Shop Till You Drop (pages 98-99)

Goodbye, Zoo! (pages 100-101)

START

EXIT

FINISH

Back to the
ZOO

Designer: Lori Bye
Art Director: Nathan Gassman
Production Specialist: Jane Klenk
The illustrations in this book were created digitally.

Picture Window Books
151 Good Counsel Drive
P.O. Box 669
Mankato, MN 56002-0669
877-845-8392
www.capstonepub.com

Printed in the United States of America in Stevens Point, Wisconsin.
082011
006349R

All books published by Picture Window Books
are manufactured with paper containing at least
10 percent post-consumer waste.

Library of Congress Cataloging-in-Publication Data

Kalz, Jill.
  A-maze-ing adventures fun finger mazes / by Jill Kalz;
illustrated by Mattia Cerato.
  p. cm.—(A-maze-ing adventures)
  ISBN 978-1-4048-6401-6 (bind up)
  1. Maze puzzles—Juvenile literature.
  2. Map reading—Juvenile literature. I. Cerato, Mattia, ill.
  II. Title. III. Title: Fun finger mazes.
  GV1507.M3K35 2011
  793.73'8—dc22   2010026486